MW01624223

Forever Home

Tales of Four Lucky Dogs

by LYNN WHITMAN

illustrated by DEB HOEFFNER

Becklyns, LLC
Weatogue, CT

Acknowledgments

This book would not have been possible without the encouragement, love, and support of Pam Whitman, Rob Whitman, and Jeff Munger. Thank you to Jennifer Wright of Labs4Rescue for suggesting I write about adopting a rescue dog. Many thanks to my editor, Rebecca Chown, for her advice and creative assistance in helping me to write even better tales. Thanks to Kristen Pawloski for her red pen. Thank you also to Leah Nicholson and Jerrold Jenkins for helping me understand the process of self-publishing a book. Thank you to Yvonne Roehler for her help with the design process. Finally, a heartfelt thank you to my illustrator, Deb Hoeffner, for her enormous talent. This book would not have happened without her.

Published by Becklyns, LLC, Weatogue, CT

Publisher's Cataloging-in-Publication Data
Whitman, Lynn.

Forever home : tales of four lucky dogs / by Lynn Whitman ; illustrated by Deb Hoeffner. – Weatogue, CT : Becklyns, LLC, 2012.

p. ; cm.

Summary: Stories of four rescue dogs in loving forever homes.

ISBN13: 978-0-9860222-0-3

1. Rescue dogs—Juvenile literature. I. Title. II. Hoeffner, Deb.

SF428.55.W45 2012
636.70886—dc23 2012947045

Project coordination by Jenkins Group, Inc.
www.BookPublishing.com

Printed in Malaysia by TWP Sdn Bhd, First Printing, September 2012
16 15 14 13 12 • 5 4 3 2 1

To

Rob, Becky, Kristen, Brian, Robby, Hailey, Aidan, Katie, Olivia,
and the boy down the street named Sam.

This book is dedicated to all who adopt dogs,
and to all dogs in need of forever homes.

Max's Tale

My name is Max. I'm a rescue dog, and my story is one of the happy ones. You know, a litter of cute fuzzy puppies gets dropped off at a humane society where they hope to be adopted by excited, loving families. Luckily, that's exactly what happened to me.

I was eight weeks old, the perfect age to leave my littermates and join my forever family, when Dad saw me at the humane society. I'd only been there two days when he asked my mom to come down and take a look at me. She was going to have a baby of her own and I knew she was thinking, "What do I need with a puppy?" But when she saw the sparkle of love in my dad's eyes, she said "Yes" and into a cat carrier I went for the ride home.

As an Akita husky puppy, it was clear I was going to be huge. What was I doing in a cat carrier?

My new home was perfect for a frisky puppy like me, and right away I found out I had an older sister, a border collie named Zoie. She was sweet, but she was also very scared. If she'd been a turtle, she would have crawled into her shell.

For a long time, Zoie kept to herself. Even though she was five years old, I intimidated her. I was full of puppy energy, and I wanted to jump and bark and wrestle. To get away from me, Zoie often hid under the bed. She even slept under the bed, but I got to sleep with Mom and Dad in their king-sized bed.

The first few weeks in my new home, Dad kept his leg over me at night, holding me down so I couldn't jump on and off the bed.

At first it took some getting used to because I wanted to play, but after I heard him tell Mom they'd have to put me in a crate at night if I didn't stay put, I decided that nighttime was for sleeping.

Soon, I was three months old. Dad decided it was time for me to attend obedience training class. It was very exciting to meet all of the new dogs at puppy school. I couldn't wait to run and play with my new friends, but we didn't have much time for that. Instead, we were taught to walk on a leash and to come when we were called and to sit and stay.

Truth be told, I wasn't the best-behaved dog in the class. The only thing I excelled at was sitting with a cookie on my nose waiting for permission to eat it. It was worth learning that trick, because I love food!

My new mom was wonderful, loving, and kind, but once the new baby was born, she didn't have as much time for me so Dad took over my grooming care. Being brushed is one thing I really don't like. I do need to be brushed—I shed a lot, have allergies and am very itchy. Dad tried his best, but I didn't make it easy for him.

As the years flew by, Mom had two more babies. I now lived with Hailey, Aidan, and Olivia the baby. None of them ever pulled my tail, and they all loved to pile on my dog bed and curl up with me. I still slept with Mom and Dad at night, but in the daytime I got cozy on a dog bed, chair, or couch.

Once, when I was about two years old, just to get Mom's attention, I ate a whole chicken she had set out for dinner. Another time, I ate a whole box of dog cookies. As naughty as I was, she didn't scold me, but I did get her attention!

Probably the worst thing I ever did was to eat a bottle of pills. Hailey was sick and Mom couldn't leave the house, so Dad had to come home from work to take me to the vet. I had to spend the night there and they made me throw up to get rid of the pills.

Note to self: do not eat a bottle of pills again.

Once Mom and Dad had a picnic for their friends and neighbors, and I took the opportunity to sneak my favorite food: hotdogs! I can look pretty innocent when I try, and I waited behind a tree in the yard for much of the party. Whenever the coast was clear, I zipped forward and grabbed one or two at a time from the picnic table. I'm so big that I just reached up and took them right off the serving platter. I never got caught, and Mom was amazed at how many hotdogs the kids ate!

I'm happy to say that Zoie and I have become great friends. She has really come out of her shell. We play in the yard, dig holes, and chase everything we see. One day I taught her how to sneak out of the yard when no one was looking and away we went. We had a great adventure, but I admit that once we left the neighborhood, I got a little scared. I didn't let on to Zoie, but we were completely lost. Luckily for me, Mom drove around until she found us. I would not have wanted to go without dinner.

I'm now eight years old. I look fierce because my eyes are two different colors, but I'm really very loveable. Ask anyone who comes to the house. I still love getting up on my hind legs and putting my paws around a visitor's neck to give them kisses. I'm happy my dad and mom brought me home from the humane society and into their loving family. Hotdogs or no hotdogs, there's no place I'd rather be.

Lila's Tale

My name is Lila, short for Delilah. My mom loves flowers. Her favorite flower is a dahlia. I think naming me Delilah was the closest she could come to that. You may think it is silly, but I think it is sweet.

I am a black lab mix and a bit on the small side. Don't tell my mom, but the other mixed part of me is pit bull. She's only heard bad stories about pit bulls. She doesn't know that they are delightful, loving, and loyal, just like black labs.

I'm a lucky girl. When I was three, I was found wandering the streets and brought to a Labs4Rescue house to stay with other dogs. I was a runaway, and I'd fled the last three homes I'd lived in. The people weren't mean—they just didn't understand me or have much time for me, and I didn't have any reason to stay.

At the rescue house, our pictures were posted on their website and we waited until someone wanted to take us home. It wasn't long before someone was interested in me, and I was glad. I might not have liked my former homes, but I didn't want to live on the streets either. My goal was to keep trying new homes until I found my forever home, so I did my best to make a good first impression.

I didn't let on that I am a true stray at heart and that, given an excuse, I'd be gone, baby, gone. I knew which side my bread was buttered on, so I gave my visitor my paw and looked at her with my head innocently cocked to one side. She took the bait hook, line, and sinker, and soon I was in a cozy loving home that seemed too good to be true.

Mom is such a dog person that before she knew it, I had the run of the place. I can do practically anything I want, including sitting on top of a great big chair in the living room. From the top of that chair, I look out the window and grunt and bark at people as they pass.

When I'm happy, I make grunting noises, and when I see people, I bark with excitement. I like to talk, and I also like my creature comforts. That's why I'm so happy that Mom has two couches. How cool is that? We both have a place to watch television or just plain nap.

Mom's a teacher at a private school, and every day I get to go with her. We take long walks during the day, and the kids are always arguing about who gets to hold my leash. It's wonderful having so much attention, and exciting things are always happening at school. Just after Thanksgiving, I found a turkey leg in a trashcan. You should have seen the looks on the children's faces as I ran around them proudly showing off my prize.

On weekends, Mom and I go on the best hikes of all, to a park where I'm allowed to run free. Well, not too free. I wear a collar, and if I don't come back when she calls, she can make a buzzer go off that signals me to come back. I don't like the buzzer, so I always come when she calls.

Mom is the first person to try the buzzer on me, and it really works. So far I haven't found an opportunity to run away, but then again, I haven't been looking for one. I really like my new mom! My favorite part of our walks is rolling in great-smelling goose poop. I find the fragrance wonderful, and I can't understand why Mom always gives me a bath when we get home!

Mom's sister has a big chocolate lab named Cocoa. She's probably three times my size, but I'm not afraid of her. Whenever we visit, Cocoa and I run in the yard together. On our last visit, she taught me how to dig for chipmunks. I have lots of other dog friends, but Cocoa seems like a big sister. I don't remember any of my canine siblings, so I'm glad to have Cocoa.

Just last week, Mom bought me a special rawhide bone to celebrate our two-year anniversary together. I can't believe I've been with Mom for two whole years already! I like her so much that now it's hard to be apart from her. Sometimes Mom has me spend the night with Cocoa, and as close as we are, the first night is always difficult. I usually lie by the door and cry, but as soon as Mom comes back, I grunt and wiggle with happiness. This makes Mom laugh, which makes me grunt even more.

I love my mom. I love our home and our life. I'm no longer a stray. I can't believe I'm saying this, but I no longer want to run away. Now, every part of me says, stay, baby, stay.

Sam's Tale

My name is Sam. I just turned twelve, which means in dog years that I'm pretty old. I'm your typical unwanted dog, and I've spent most of my life in animal shelters.

I'm a good dog—I never bite and I get along with others—but mine is a hard luck story. The dad in my first family lost his job when I was about a year old and the family couldn't afford to keep me. I've been in and out of shelters ever since. I was briefly adopted by really nice people, but the economy hasn't worked in my favor and I ended up back in a shelter.

Up until a few months ago, I lived in a cage on a cold cement floor in a pretty typical animal shelter. It's hard to believe, but I lived there five whole years. It was okay as far as shelters go, but it was still a shelter. I didn't belong to anyone and no one belonged to me.

I was taken outside twice every day to relieve myself, but those outdoor excursions were short. I never had time to sniff or play, and the yard I was taken into was ugly with debris and the grass was brown and worn. Those brief outings aside, I seldom had a chance to stand up or run around and my legs became weak from lying down so much.

I don't know why the shelter kept me so long. City shelters don't have a lot of money, so if no one adopts you, your days are numbered. The fact is, most people who come to a shelter want a puppy. Day after day, visitors would glance at my cage and then walk on by. It always hurt, but I got used to it. At my age, I never expected to be wanted again.

I didn't have to look in the mirror to know I was the complete opposite of an appealing little puppy. I was bony, my fur was thin, my teeth were brown, and my muzzle had turned gray. Also, I was nothing special – only a mutt, a mix of border collie, Australian shepherd, and who knows what else.

You can imagine my surprise when a kind-looking woman came into the shelter one day and said she was interested in adopting an older dog. I painfully got to my feet for our introduction and then sat right down beside her.

My new mom-to-be was taken with what she thought was our immediate bond and she began to ask questions.

How old is he?

Does he have any health problems?

Can he climb stairs?

What is his background?

She was told that I was ten, in good health, that climbing stairs wasn't a problem, and that I'd been in and out of city shelters all my life. They also told her I was such a calm, kind dog that they hadn't had the heart to put me down, even though I held the record for the longest time at the shelter.

That did it. My new mom told me I was the dog for her and that she was going to take me home and love me for the rest of my life. I was so old and tired that it was hard to believe anything good could happen to me, but I managed to wag my tail to show her how happy I was.

As soon as we left the shelter, my new mom realized that things weren't quite as true as she'd been told. When she had to help me into the car, she knew that my hips and back legs didn't work very well. She understood that was why I'd sat down beside her at the shelter. When she checked my paperwork, her suspicions about my real age were confirmed.

To my great relief, this kind and loving lady didn't reject me, instead, she took my muzzle in her hands and told me my special needs only made her want me more. While she gently stroked my head, she told me that she needed me too. Can you imagine that?

It had been a long time since I'd been looked at with pride or touched with loving hands. As soon as we arrived at my new home, she gave me a bath and brushed me with a brush that didn't hurt my bony hips at all. I hadn't had a bath in years, and it felt wonderful to have my coat massaged, my ears cleaned, and my toenails trimmed.

While I dried, my new mom fed me from my very own bowl, took me out for a slow, gentle walk in a sweet-smelling yard, and then showed me to a brand new bed. I sank down into the thick, comfortable nest with a grateful sigh and shuddered at the thought of the cold cement floor I'd recently left. My life had clearly changed for the better, but I was a little confused.

I think my new mom knew how I felt, because she sat on the floor with me and stroked my ears. She told me I was a good dog and that she loved me over and over again. Her hand felt so good that I fell asleep.

As the days went by and her loving care never wavered, I began to feel a real bond with her. With excellent care, a comfortable bed, and many excursions outside every day, I also began to gain strength. Soon the best part of my day was going outside on our frequent walks. My new mom would pick up my red leash and say, "Ready for a walk, Sam?"

I was always game, even when my hips hurt. I just couldn't get enough fresh air and sunshine. Mom always put me on a leash, but she didn't need to. I was better, but I still couldn't walk very far or very fast.

It was wonderful to feel the grass under my paws and to see squirrels chattering and chasing each other in the yard. If I'd been a little bit younger, I would have tried to chase them myself.

Often, when the days were warm, Mom would bring a book outside and sit on a bench to read. I would curl up in the grass beside her or lie under a giant oak tree and watch the birds and smell the wind.

It was a pleasant surprise to learn I wasn't the only Sam in the neighborhood. On a walk one day, the boy down the street came up to meet me and I learned his name was also Sam. Whenever Mom and I were out walking, he would come out to say hi and pat me on the head.

Sharing a name with Sam made me feel special. The other children in the neighborhood would pat me too, but they usually commented on how old I was or how my breath smelled bad. Sam didn't seem to care about any of that.

In spite of the wonderful care I now receive, I'm not in good shape. My body rallied for a short time, but my age has caught up with me. Several months after I was adopted, my legs began collapsing under me. Whenever I fall, my new mom patiently waits for me to regain my footing. She understands my need for dignity even when she has to help me back up. She knows I like gazing into her eyes, and she likes gazing into mine, too.

I wish I could slow down time. I don't want to leave this new and wonderful life. It took me a long time to find someone to love me, but being adopted was worth the wait.

Cocoa's Tale

MY NAME IS COCOA. I am a chocolate lab. Seven years ago, I was a stray living on the streets in New Orleans. I was alone, hungry, and scared. I'd lost my family in a terrible hurricane that nearly destroyed the entire city. After several scary, lonely weeks, I was found by some nice people who took me to a Labs4Rescue center. At the center, they fed me and found a new home for me miles away in Connecticut.

Lots of other dogs made the three-day trip to Connecticut with me. I'm a big dog and I didn't have to be put in a cage for the trip, but just because I'm big doesn't mean I felt brave. I was scared, and I missed my family terribly. I knew I would never see them again, and I wondered what would become of me.

We arrived on a cold February day. One by one the dogs were let out of their cages and introduced to their new families. Finally, it was my turn to meet my new mom, and right away I had a good feeling about her. She spoke to me very gently and seemed to understand that I was fragile inside.

I liked my new house, too, though at first I was very timid about entering any rooms. I especially liked the big fenced yard. The beautiful stone wall on the inside of the fence gave me a feeling of security. I could run around all I liked, but I couldn't run away and I couldn't get lost. It made me feel safe. Though I hadn't yet bonded with my new mom, I was so insecure that I didn't want to let her out of my sight.

Mom seemed to understand. She fed me twice a day, took me on long walks, and gave me rides in the car with the window down so I could breathe the fresh air. She kept telling me she loved me and that she would take care of me, but I was too scared to show her any love back.

After a week or so in my new home, I gathered my courage and jumped into bed with my new mom. I hoped she would let me stay, and maybe because I was trembling, she did. She realized that even though I was big and seemed confident, I needed a lot of love. Soon, I was even sitting in her lap while we watched television. This might sound reasonable, but remember, I'm a big girl. I weigh almost one hundred pounds.

Mom likes to garden, so that means we're outside a lot. That's fine with me, because our yard is full of chipmunks that I love to chase. They live in the ground, so I dig holes to try to catch them. Often, the chipmunks run into the stone wall, and I stick my nose in, nudge around, and flip the rocks onto the ground. Sometimes I skin my nose a little, but it always heals fast, and Mom doesn't seem to mind replacing the rocks in the stone wall every now and then.

deb

Sometimes my cousin comes over to play. Lila is younger than me and I had to teach her how to dig holes, but she's really good at it now. I love playing with my cousin.

Lila's a lot smaller than me, but she's game for anything and she has this funny way of grunting that I kind of enjoy. I love chasing chipmunks with Lila or by myself, but what I really want to do is chase a squirrel.

One time I cut one of my toes while digging in the stone wall and Mom had to take me to the vet. I almost cried when I learned that I would have to stay overnight. Yikes, no lap, no television, and no big bed! I was scared to be separated from Mom, but she told me she would come back to get me the next day, and she did. My paw was still sore, but I didn't care because I was going home!

One day, when Mom and I were taking a walk, I saw a squirrel and saw my chance. Before Mom knew it, I had slipped out of my collar and was running through the woods. It was pure bliss. I'd forgotten what running as fast as you can for as long as you want feels like! I was having so much fun I didn't realize I was lost. Soon it was dark, but I have such a good sense of smell that it only took me a little while to find my way home.

I thought I would be in a lot of trouble, but Mom stroked me and told me how happy she was to see me. She even told me that leaving her side to chase a squirrel meant my confidence was coming back. It sounds kind of funny, but she told me this meant I was getting over the terrible trauma of losing my first family.

I think Mom is right, but I also know that in my heart, I'm still a timid girl who needs her mom close by to feel safe and happy. As time goes by, I am more and more confident, but I'll never stop wanting to be near Mom. Wherever she goes, I go, even into the laundry room, the basement, or the bathroom. I love to be with her, no matter what she's doing.

It's a good feeling to know what's ahead for me: long walks, frequent rides in the car, chipmunks to chase (and maybe the occasional squirrel), play dates with Lila, and lots of snuggle time with Mom. I'm a happy dog, and life is good. Thanks to Mom, I'm not nearly as scared as I used to be, and I'll probably always be a lap dog at heart.

About the Author

LYNN WHITMAN, a vocal advocate for rescue dogs, lives in Connecticut, where she is never without the companionship of a dog. When she isn't working in the finance department at the Jones Companies, Whitman enjoys spending time with her grown children and five wonderful grandchildren. *Forever Home* was written for those who love and rescue dogs.

About the Illustrator

DEB HOEFFNER describes her unique style of "soft realism" as a layering of thought, paint, and possibilities. An award-winning artist and illustrator whose work has been widely published over a thirty-year career, she specializes in capturing the spirit of her subjects with expressions that tell tales. Books illustrated by Deb include *A Dog's Guide to Life: Lessons from Moose* by Jack Cotton, the award-winning children's book *All You Want and Then Some* by Carolyn McWilliams Brown, and most recently, *Lucky: The Tale of a Tree* by Richard C. Hawkins. She shares her studio in Bucks County, Pennsylvania, with her dog Emma. More of her work can be seen at www.debhoeffner.com.

Cover illustration in progress on Deb's drawing table. Her tools include watercolors, pencils, brushes, and most importantly a photo of Lila for inspiration.